divine
desserts

divine desserts

tessa bramley

photography by christine hanscomb

RYLAND
PETERS
& SMALL
LONDON NEW YORK

Designer	Luis Peral-Aranda
Commissioning Editor	Elsa Petersen-Schepelern
Editors	Maddalena Bastianelli
	Jennifer Herman
Production	Patricia Harrington
Art Director	Gabriella Le Grazie
Publishing Director	Alison Starling
Food Stylist	Maxine Clark
Stylist	Antonia Gaunt
Photographer's Assistant	Teresa Cotterell

First published in the United States in 2002
by Ryland Peters & Small, Inc.
519 Broadway, 5th Floor
New York, NY 10012
www.rylandpeters.com

10 9 8 7 6 5 4 3 2 1

Text © Tessa Bramley 2002
Design and photographs
© Ryland Peters & Small 2002

ISBN 1 84172 282 0

Library of Congress Cataloging-in-Publication Data
Bramley, Tessa.
    Divine desserts / by Tessa Bramley.
        p. cm.
    Includes index.
    ISBN 1-84172-282-0
        1. Desserts. I. Title.
    TX773 .B7453 2002
    641.8'6—dc21   2001048860

Printed and bound in China

Dedication and Acknowledgments

I dedicate this book with special thanks to my brother, Howard, whose love of desserts is legendary and whose sweet tooth inspired me. I hope you like it Howard.

Thanks to my mum whose pastry was exemplary, to Andrew, Carole, and Linda who believe in me and support me, and of course, posthumously, to Sarah, my grandma, who set me on the right track all those years ago. My thanks to Nathan and Caroline for testing and tasting the recipes and to Andrew for keeping things ticking over whilst we played! I am indebted to Elsa at Ryland Peters & Small for patiently urging me on, for her boundless enthusiasm for the subject, and for producing such a lovely book.

Notes

All spoon measurements are level unless otherwise stated.

All eggs are large, unless otherwise specified. Uncooked or partially cooked eggs should not be served to the very young, the very old, those with compromised immune systems, or to pregnant women.

Several recipes in this book use self-rising flour. If unavailable, use all-purpose flour plus extra baking powder in the ratio of 2 teaspoons baking powder to each 1¾ cups of flour.

Preheat ovens to the specified temperature. These recipes were tested with a regular oven. If using a convection oven, decrease the cooking times according to the manufacturer's instructions.

Recipes in this book were tested using best quality cooking chocolate, at least 55–60 percent cocoa solids. When melting chocolate, put it into a heatproof bowl set over a saucepan of simmering water. Do not let the water touch the base of the bowl. Melt gently—do not let any water or steam touch the chocolate, or it will turn into an unusable lump.

Recipes in this book use whole vanilla beans or best quality vanilla extract. Vanilla beans, though expensive, can be reused, even after they have been split and the seeds removed. Just dry them off with paper towels and store in an airtight jar of superfine or confectioner's sugar, to make vanilla sugar.

Sterilizing preserving jars Wash the jars in hot, soapy water and rinse in boiling water. Put into a large saucepan and cover with hot water. With the lid on, bring the water to a boil and continue boiling for 15 minutes. Turn off the heat, then leave the jars in the hot water until just before they are to be filled. Invert the jars onto a clean cloth to dry. Sterilize the lids for 5 minutes, by boiling or according to the manufacturer's instructions. The jars should be filled and sealed while they are still hot. For useful guidelines on preserving, see website http://hgic.clemson.edu/factsheets/HGIC3040.htm.

contents

the perfect finale ...

A dessert is an unequivocal luxury. It takes time and loving care to make. Intensely fruity, luscious and creamy, or buttery and gloriously decadent, desserts and self indulgence go hand in hand.

When she was young, my grandma, Sarah, was a parlormaid in a grand Victorian household. She always taught me that desserts should be lavishly produced from the best ingredients—she firmly believed in the "wow!" factor. From her I learned about spices and flavorings, about the importance of using unsalted butter for baking (she would call it "sweet" butter), and about serving desserts with a flourish. It was the proud gleam in her eye when she presented her wonderful pear and almond tart which added to its enjoyment: it was a simple presentation, just pure ground almonds with a beautiful sticky glaze, yet a sublime experience.

She showed me how to take pleasure in the feel and scent of ingredients—that the purest flavor of a lemon is in the oil of the zest. We spent some happy mornings rubbing the lemon skins all over with sugar lumps to extract the intense flavor, all ready to make her famous lemon curd before baking day started. The sugar acted as a very fine grater removing the surface lemon color, tinting the sugar yellow, and at the same time absorbing the lemon oil to give the curd we made with it a clear and zingy citrus tang.

Some of the desserts in this book are outrageously luxurious, while others are simple and comforting—but all are created with love for you to enjoy.

baked
desserts

Very simple, very light, and impossible to resist, this old-fashioned dessert has always been one of the most popular we have ever served at The Old Vicarage. To "gild the lily," I like to top each one with a chocolate heart. The chocolate melts into the hot fudge sauce, leaving a pale, matte impression on the glossy surface. Easy and stylish for a special occasion.

baked chocolate dessert
with chocolate fudge sauce and custard

1¼ cups self-rising flour (see page 4)

1 teaspoon baking powder

½ teaspoon baking soda

2 heaping tablespoons unsweetened cocoa powder

¾ cup sugar

2 extra-large eggs, beaten

2 tablespoons corn syrup

¾ cup milk

¾ cup safflower oil

Chocolate fudge sauce

7 oz. bitter (baking) chocolate

1 cup heavy cream

2½ cups confectioners' sugar, sifted

To serve

Chocolate Hearts (optional)*

1 recipe hot Quick Vanilla Custard (see page 62)

8 small ramekins or custard cups, ¾ cup each, greased

Serves 8

To make the pudding, sift the flour, baking powder, baking soda, cocoa powder, and sugar into a mixing bowl. Make a well in the center. Pour the beaten eggs into the well, then add the corn syrup, milk, and oil. Using a balloon whisk, gradually draw in the dry ingredients from the sides of the bowl and beat to make a smooth batter.

Pour the mixture into the prepared molds and bake in a preheated oven at 300°F for about 30 minutes, until springy to the touch.

To make the fudge sauce, put the chocolate and cream into the top of a double boiler and melt gently over a medium heat. Alternatively, use a heatproof bowl set over a saucepan of steaming water. Gradually beat in the confectioners' sugar until the sauce is glossy and all the sugar has dissolved.

To serve, unmold the puddings onto small plates and pour the hot custard around the puddings. Pour the fudge sauce over the top and serve immediately.

*Chocolate Hearts Put about 2 squares (2 oz.) bittersweet chocolate into a heatproof bowl set over a saucepan of simmering water. Do not let the water touch the base of the bowl. Heat until melted. Pour the melted chocolate onto a sheet of parchment paper and let it set. Cut out little heart shapes using a petits fours cutter. Put one on top of each dessert just before serving. The hot fudge sauce will melt the heart, leaving a slightly lighter impression on top of the dessert.

A very light, fresh, and lemony pudding with a zingy lemon sauce— it couldn't be simpler. I think it's even better with a little pool of homemade custard (page 62), but then I am a custard fan!

baked lemon dessert
with lemon butter sauce

**1½ cups self-rising flour
(see page 4)**

1½ teaspoons baking powder

a pinch of salt

¾ cup sugar

finely grated zest of 2 lemons

3 large eggs, beaten

**1 stick plus 5 tablespoons
unsalted butter, melted,
then cooled**

3 drops of lemon oil

**⅓ cup milk mixed
with ⅓ cup cold water**

**Quick Candied Lemon Zest,
to serve (optional)***

Lemon butter sauce

⅓ cup sugar

**finely grated zest and juice
of 2 lemons, plus the juice
of 1 extra lemon**

2 tablespoons Cointreau

**1 stick unsalted butter,
cut into cubes and chilled**

*6 individual ramekins or custard
cups, greased, then dredged with
a mixture of flour and sugar*

Serves 6

To make the dessert, sift the flour, baking powder, salt, and sugar into a bowl and stir in the zest. Make a well in the center and add the eggs, butter, lemon oil, and milk mixture. Mix with a small whisk to form a smooth batter.

Pour into the prepared ramekins and bake in a preheated oven at 350°F for about 20–25 minutes, until well risen and golden. The desserts should feel as firm in the middle as they do at the sides. Turn the ramekins upside down onto a wire cooling rack and let cool for 5 minutes. Ease a small knife around the sides of the ramekins to loosen each dessert, then gently shake out.

To make the sauce, put the sugar and lemon juice into a small, nonreactive (stainless steel or enamel) saucepan and dissolve gently over a low heat. Add the lemon zest and bring to a boil. Cook at a fast bubble for 2–3 minutes to reduce the liquid to a thick syrup. Remove from the heat and strain out the zest. Add the Cointreau, then beat in the chilled butter, a little at a time, until the sauce is thickened and glossy.

Serve with the sauce poured over and around each dessert. A little pile of candied zest on top adds crunch and tangy freshness.

*Quick Candied Lemon Zest Using a lemon zester or cannelle knife, remove long, fine strips of zest from 1 lemon. Put into a saucepan of cold water and bring to a boil to soften the strips. Drain, then dry the zest with paper towels. Transfer to a small saucepan, add 2 tablespoons sugar, and toss over the heat until the sugar has stuck to the lemon and formed a candied coating. Store in a little box of sugar until needed.

Choose your favorite berries or perhaps peaches for this orange sponge pudding. The recipe can change with the seasons— although I think the deep purple of blueberries and blackberries make it particularly attractive. I used blueberries and cherries this time, but would avoid strawberries.

blueberry and cherry sponge

1 lb. mixed fruit, such as pitted cherries and blueberries, about 3 cups

½ cup plus 3 tablespoons sugar

1 cup self-rising flour (see page 4)

a pinch of salt

1 teaspoon baking powder

1¼ sticks unsalted butter, softened

2 large eggs, lightly beaten

finely grated zest of 1 orange

1 recipe hot Quick Vanilla Custard (see page 62) or cream, to serve

5-cup ceramic bowl, greased, then dredged with a mixture of all-purpose flour and sugar

Serves 6–8

Reserve ½ cup of the fruit and 1 tablespoon of the sugar. Mix the remaining fruit with 2 tablespoons of the sugar, then transfer to the prepared ceramic bowl.

Sift the flour, salt, and baking powder into a second bowl.

Put the softened butter and the remaining ½ cup sugar into a mixing bowl and beat with a wooden spoon until very light, fluffy, and creamy in color. Add the eggs, a little at a time, beating between each addition, until the mixture is light and fluffy. Add the orange zest.

Sift half the flour mixture over the butter mixture and lightly fold in the flour with a metal spoon. Repeat with the remaining flour, taking care not to overmix: the mixture should drop softly off the spoon. If it is too stiff, fold in about 1 tablespoon water to make a soft dropping consistency.

Spoon the mixture over the fruit, starting at the edges and working towards the center. Smooth the top, making a slight indentation with the spoon in the middle so the mixture will rise evenly.

Bake in a preheated oven at 350°F for 30–35 minutes until golden, well risen and as firm in the middle as it is at the sides. Remove from the oven and let settle a little before turning out onto a serving dish.

To make the sauce, put the reserved fruit and sugar into a blender and blend to a smooth purée. Serve the sponge with sauce and cream or custard.

apricot bread and butter puddings

Light and wobbly bread and butter pudding is true nursery food. Rather than the more usual dried fruits, I prefer to use tangy apricots, which I think counterbalance the creaminess of the custard. Served with a sharp, fresh apricot sauce, this comforting dessert makes an altogether more elegant dish, fit for a dinner party.

1 vanilla bean, split lengthwise and seeds scraped out

2 cups milk

2 cups heavy cream

5 extra-large eggs

½ cup sugar

grated zest of 1 lemon

unsalted butter, for spreading

8 slices brioche

6–8 dried apricots, chopped

a sprinkling of brown sugar, for topping

Apricot purée

8 oz. pitted fresh apricots, about 1 cup

juice of 1 lemon

½ cup sugar

1 tablespoon apricot brandy or brandy

6 small ovenproof dishes or ramekins, or 1 large dish, about 6 x 8 x 3 inches deep

a baking sheet

Serves 6

To make the custard, put the milk, cream, and vanilla bean and seeds into a large saucepan and bring to a boil.

Put the eggs and sugar into a large bowl and whisk until frothy. Gradually beat the hot vanilla cream into the eggs: the mixture will start to thicken lightly. Remove from the heat and stir in the lemon zest.

Lightly butter the brioche. Arrange half the brioche, butter side up, in the ramekins. Sprinkle half the chopped apricots over the top. Gently pour the vanilla custard over the top, letting it soak into the brioche. Sprinkle with the remaining apricots, top with the rest of the brioche, butter side up, and gently pour in the remaining custard, so that it comes to the top of the ramekins.

Stand the ramekins on a baking sheet (which is easier to lift in and out of the oven) and cook in a preheated oven at 250°F for 45 minutes, until the custard is just set but still slightly wobbly.

Meanwhile, to make the purée, put the apricots into a saucepan, add the lemon juice, sugar, brandy, and about ¼ cup water and simmer until the fruit has softened, about 10–15 minutes. Transfer to a blender and purée until smooth. Taste and add extra lemon juice or sugar to taste. The amount of water will depend on how juicy the fruits are—if the purée looks too thick, add a little more. (If using dried apricots, increase the amount of water to ⅔ cup.)

Remove the puddings from the oven, sprinkle with the brown sugar, and brown under a preheated broiler or with a blowtorch, until the top caramelizes to a crisp golden brown. Serve with the apricot purée.

coffee hazelnut desserts
with coffee bean sauce

Coffee and hazelnuts make a delicious marriage of flavors. You might also like to serve it with a simple orange compote (below).

2½ oz. hazelnuts, about ⅓ cup

½ cup self-rising flour
(see page 4)

½ teaspoon baking powder

a pinch of salt

1 stick plus 1 tablespoon
unsalted butter, softened

½ cup brown sugar

finely grated zest of 1 orange

2 teaspoons coffee syrup

2 large eggs, beaten

Coffee bean sauce

1 cup sugar

½ cup strong black coffee made
with freshly ground beans

⅓ cup heavy cream

To serve (optional)

a few coffee beans

1–2 tablespoons
Scotch whiskey

candied orange zest, to serve
(variation on Quick Candied
Lemon Zest, page 10)

*4 ramekins or custard cups, ⅔ cup,
buttered and lined with wax paper*

Serves 4

To make the desserts, put the hazelnuts into a blender and grind until chunky. Transfer to a bowl, then stir in the flour, baking powder, and salt.

Put the butter, sugar, orange zest, and coffee into a second bowl and beat until light and fluffy (use an electric mixer if you have one). Gradually beat the eggs into the mixture. Carefully fold in the flour mixture until evenly mixed. It should have a soft dropping consistency. Divide the batter between the prepared ramekins or custard cups and bake in a preheated oven at 325°F for about 25 minutes, or until well risen and firm to the touch.

Meanwhile, to make the coffee bean sauce, put the sugar into a saucepan, add 5 tablespoons water, and dissolve over a low heat. As the liquid becomes clear, increase the heat and bring to a boil. Cook, without stirring, until the sugar forms a golden caramel. Remove from the heat and carefully add the coffee (the caramel will splutter, so protect your hand with a cloth). Return to the heat and add the cream. Continue stirring until the mixture is smooth, then let simmer until reduced to a coating consistency. Remove from the heat, then add the coffee beans and whiskey to taste.

Run a little knife around the desserts and turn out carefully onto serving plates. Pour the sauce over and around, and serve with the orange compote. If you like, you can garnish the desserts with candied orange zest (see page 10).

Orange Compote Put the zest of 2 oranges into a saucepan, cover with water, and bring to a boil. Drain. Cut out the orange segments. Put ¼ cup sugar into a saucepan, add ¼ cup water, and simmer until reduced by half. Add the drained zest and orange segments, and chill until ready to serve.

pies and tarts

old-fashioned
apple and cinnamon pie

What could be better than a simple apple pie, with delicious, crisp pie crust and spicy sweet apples, just hot from the oven?

2 recipes Old Vic Foolproof Pie Crust (page 63)

Apple filling

2 teaspoons semolina or fine cornmeal

1½ lb. cooking apples, about 4 large, peeled, cored, and fairly thickly sliced

¼ cup sugar, plus extra for sprinkling

2 cinnamon sticks, broken into tiny pieces to release the flavor, or 1 teaspoon ground

whipped cream or ice cream, to serve (optional)

a deep pie dish, 10 inches diameter

Serves 4

Prepare a double recipe of pie crust dough, cover with plastic wrap, and chill in the refrigerator for about 1 hour. Cut off just a little less than half the dough, roll out, and use to line the base of the pie dish. Sprinkle with the semolina: this mops up the excess juices from the fruit, making a sauce that prevents the dough becoming soggy. Cover and chill the remaining dough until ready to use.

Fill the lined pie dish with layers of apple, sprinkling sugar and cinnamon between the layers. You will have lots of fruit, but use it all—mound it up in the center of the dish, because the apples will fall during baking. The aim is a very full, generous-looking finished pie.

Roll out the remaining dough, lift carefully with the pin, and gently ease it over the fruit, taking care not to stretch the dough. Moisten the edges with water and press the dough onto the bottom layer around the edge of the dish. Trim off any excess with a sharp knife. Tap the edges together with the back of a knife, then pinch or flute the edges together with your fingers or a fork. Using kitchen shears, snip the top of the pie in several places to let the steam escape as it cooks.

Bake in a preheated oven at 400°F for 25 minutes to crisp the pie crust, then lower the temperature to 375°F and bake for a further 40–50 minutes, until the crust and fruit are cooked through (you will need to test it with a skewer). After the first 30 minutes, you can gently rest a piece of folded parchment paper over the pie to stop it browning too much.

As soon as you take it from the oven, sprinkle with sugar so it sticks to the hot crust. Let cool a little, then serve with whipped cream or ice cream.

caramelized apple tartlets

French apple tarts always look very stylish and are scrumptious. It's a good idea to use regular apples for the topping because they hold their shape better and don't need much extra sugar.

1 recipe Old Vic Foolproof
Pie Crust (page 63)

½ recipe Pastry Cream
(page 26)

confectioners' sugar,
for dusting

tiny fresh bay leaves,
to serve (optional)

Apple purée

2 large cooking apples, about
1 lb., peeled, cored, and sliced

1½ tablespoons sugar

1 strip of lemon zest

1 tablespoon Calvados

Apple topping

1 tablespoon sugar

1 tablespoon unsalted butter

4 red apples, peeled, cored,
and thinly sliced*

*6 tartlet pans, 4 inches diameter,
or one false-bottom fluted
tart pan, 8 inches diameter*

*foil and baking beans
or uncooked rice*

Serves 6

To make the apple purée, put the apples into a saucepan, add the sugar, lemon zest, and 2 tablespoons water, bring to a boil, and simmer until cooked to a thick, dry purée. Add the Calvados and taste for sweetness, adding a little more sugar if necessary. Chill until needed.

Meanwhile, make the pie crust dough and roll out on a floured surface to ¼ inch thick. Cut the dough into 6, line the pans, and chill as described on page 63.

Line with foil and fill with baking beans or uncooked rice. Bake in a preheated oven at 400°F for about 15 minutes. (This is called blind baking.) Remove the foil and beans, lower the oven temperature to 350°F and return the pie crust to the oven for a further 5 minutes, until the crust is cooked through. Increase the oven temperature to 425°F.

To make the apple topping, heat 1 tablespoon water in a small saucepan and add the sugar and butter. Bring to a boil. Add the apple slices and cook for 2–3 minutes, until softened slightly and coated with the buttery syrup.

Divide the pastry cream between the tartlets and top with 1 tablespoon of the apple purée. Arrange overlapping apple slices on top of the apple purée to cover the surface completely. Bake in the preheated oven for 7–8 minutes, until the edges of the apple slices are deep golden and caramelized. Lightly dredge with confectioners' sugar, top with a tiny bay leaf, and serve.

*Note** The large tart uses 4 apples, the tartlets use 3.

A fabulous yet simple alternative to the classic lemon meringue pie. I use crisp apples which break down to a coarse purée, because I prefer to have some texture in the filling. You could, of course, use cooking apples, but then you must increase the sugar in the purée. If you don't like cardamom, use three or four cloves instead, but remove after making the filling.

apple amber

1 recipe Old Vic Foolproof
Pie Crust (page 63)

8 large apples, peeled,
cored, and chopped

3 strips of lemon zest
and freshly squeezed
juice of ½ lemon

seeds from 12 crushed green
cardamom pods

2–3 tablespoons sugar, or to
taste (leave slightly tart
because of the sweetness
of the meringue)

3 extra-large egg yolks

Meringue topping

3 extra-large egg whites

a pinch of salt

1¾ cups plus 2 tablespoons
superfine sugar,
plus extra for sprinkling

2 teaspoons cornstarch

2 teaspoons lemon juice

*a false-bottom tart pan,
8 inches diameter*

*foil and baking beans
or uncooked rice*

Serves 8–10

Make the pie crust dough, use to line the tart pan, and blind bake as described on page 63. Let cool while you make the filling. Reduce the oven temperature to 225°F. (Make sure it has cooled to this temperature before completing baking.)

To make the filling, put the apples, lemon zest and juice, cardamom seeds, sugar, and 3 tablespoons water into a saucepan and cook over moderate heat until softened to a coarse pulp. Remove and discard the strips of lemon zest.

Put the 3 egg yolks into a bowl, beat well, then stir into the apple purée. Pour the mixture into the cooked and cooled pie crust.

To make the meringue topping, put the egg whites and salt into a clean, dry bowl and, using a balloon whisk, beat until stiff. Beat in 1 tablespoon of the remaining sugar until the mixture is glossy and standing in stiff peaks. Beat in the remaining sugar in 2 batches, beating back to stiff peaks after each addition. Sprinkle with the cornstarch and lemon juice and fold in gently (I like to use the whisk for folding).

Using a large spoon, pile the meringue on top of the apple filling. Sprinkle about 1 tablespoon sugar over the top. Bake in the cool oven for about 1 hour until the meringue is crisp on the outside with the peaks just tinged golden. The center of the meringue will be fluffy and marshmallow-like.

pear and almond frangipane tart

A tart that looks spectacular, but is simple and inexpensive to make. You could use almost any kind of fruit—it also works well with plums and fresh apricots. With its light texture, it's best eaten on the day it's made, but does freeze very well. However, do serve it warm.

1 recipe Old Vic Foolproof Pie Crust (page 63)

⅓ cup apricot jam

1 stick plus 2 tablespoons unsalted butter, softened

½ cup sugar

2 large eggs, beaten

1 tablespoon self-rising flour (see page 4)

Following the recipe on page 63, make the pie crust dough, use to line the prepared tart pan, and blind bake. Let the crust cool, but keep the oven at 350°F.

Spread about 2½ tablespoons of the jam into the cooked pie crust. Put the remaining 3½ tablespoons into a small saucepan, add 2–3 tablespoons water, and bring to a boil. Strain to remove any pieces of fruit. (This is the glaze for painting the tart before serving.)

1 teaspoon baking powder

½ cup ground almonds, or ¾ cup blanched almonds, ground in a blender

3 almost-ripe pears, peeled, halved, and cored

a rectangular false-bottom tart pan, about 13 x 4 inches, or a round tart pan, 11-inches diameter

foil and baking beans or uncooked rice

Serves 4–6

Put the butter and sugar into a bowl, then beat until light and fluffy. Add the beaten eggs, a little at a time, beating well until the mixture is very light.

Sift the flour and baking powder into a separate bowl and stir in the ground almonds. Fold the flour mixture lightly into the butter mixture—it will drop softly off the spoon. Spread evenly over the jam in the pie crust.

Put the pear halves cut side down onto a chopping board. With a sharp knife, slice the pears lengthwise, leaving the stem end still intact. Press down on the fruit with the flat of your hand so the slices fan out. Using a spatula, lift the pear fans onto the tart. Arrange the stem ends towards the center if you are making a round tart, or set alternately, top to tail, if using a rectangular pan.

Bake in the preheated oven for about 40–50 minutes until the almond filling is well risen and feels firm in the middle. To test, insert a skewer into the almond filling: it should come out clean. Brush with the apricot glaze and serve warm.

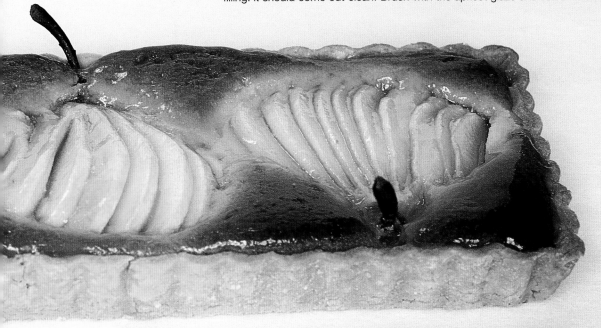

raspberry tart with caramel almonds

A spectacular dinner-party finale with a shortbread crust. The caramel shards add special drama, but, for a more casual occasion, omit them and fill the space with more raspberries.

1¼ sticks unsalted butter

5 tablespoons sugar

¾ cup all-purpose flour

⅓ cup semolina

1 lb. raspberries, about 3 cups

Caramel almond shards

10 blanched almonds, chopped

¾ cup superfine sugar

Pastry cream

4 large egg yolks

2 tablespoons all-purpose flour

1 teaspoon cornstarch

2 tablespoons sugar

2¾ cups light cream

1 vanilla bean, split lengthwise

1 tablespoon ground almonds, or 2 tablespoons blanched almonds, ground in a blender

1 tablespoon framboise (raspberry) liqueur, or brandy

a baking sheet, lined with parchment paper

a false-bottom tart pan, 10 inches diameter

foil and baking beans or uncooked rice

Serves 4–6

To make the shortbread pie crust dough, put the butter and sugar into a bowl and beat until creamy. Put the flour and semolina into a second bowl and mix well. Gradually beat in the butter mixture to form a crumbly dough. Transfer to a floured work surface and knead carefully until it comes together smoothly. As described in the recipe on page 63, roll out to line the flan tin, chill for 1 hour, then blind bake in a preheated oven at 300°F for 20 minutes. Let cool.

To make the caramel almond shards, sprinkle the prepared baking sheet with the chopped nuts. Put the sugar into a heavy saucepan, add 3 tablespoons water, and heat gently until the sugar dissolves. Boil rapidly until it forms a golden caramel. Pour over the nuts and let cool completely. When cold and set, gently tap the caramel and break it into shards. Reserve.

To make the pastry cream, put the egg yolks, flour, cornstarch, and sugar into a bowl and whisk until blended. Put the cream into a saucepan, add the vanilla bean and seeds, and bring to a boil. Pour the hot cream onto the egg mixture, and beat vigorously.

Pour into a bowl, rinse the saucepan, return the mixture to the pan, and cook gently over low heat, stirring all the time until it thickly coats the back of a spoon.

Remove and discard the vanilla bean and stir in the ground almonds and liqueur. Pour the pastry cream into the cooked pie crust. Let cool completely.

When cool, arrange the raspberries neatly on top of the pastry cream, leaving the center clear. Pile the center of the tart with the glossy shards of caramelized almonds. Serve.

A deliciously rich yet fragile pie crust dough that must be well chilled before you attempt to roll it out. I make the dough the day before I need it and keep it in the refrigerator. The semolina thickens the fruit juices during baking, making a lovely syrupy sauce.

blackberry, apple, and orange deep dish

3 oz. full-fat cream cheese, ⅓ cup

6 tablespoons unsalted butter, softened

1 cup all-purpose flour

Fruit filling

1 tablespoon unsalted butter

1 lb. Granny Smith apples, about 3, peeled, cored, and sliced

2 tablespoons semolina

⅓ cup sugar

grated zest and juice of 3 oranges

1 lb. blackberries or loganberries, about 3½ cups

confectioners' sugar, for dusting

Orange cream (optional)

1 cup heavy cream

2 teaspoons confectioners' sugar

grated zest of 1 orange

an oval or round deep pie dish, about 8 inches diameter

Serves 6

To make the pie crust dough, put the cream cheese and butter into a bowl and beat until light and fluffy. Add the flour gradually, beating into the dough until it is well blended. Wrap in plastic wrap and chill until needed.

To make the filling, dice the butter, put it into a large saucepan, and heat until melted. Add the apple slices, turning them in the butter to coat. Put the semolina onto a plate. Remove the apples from the pan and toss in the semolina.

Put the sugar, orange zest and juice, and 1 tablespoon water into a saucepan, bring to a boil, then reduce to a syrup. Put the apples into the pie dish, add the blackberries, and mix gently. Pour over the orange syrup and let cool.

Put the dough onto a lightly floured work top. Roll out carefully and evenly to a shape about 1 inch larger than the top of the pie dish. Cut to shape and use the trimmings to make a thin layer round the top edge of the dish. Moisten with a little water.

Using the rolling pin to help you, ease the dough over the top of the dish. Press the edges of the 2 layers of dough firmly together. Either crimp or flute the edge of the dough using your fingers. Make several vents in the top of the dough lid to let the steam escape as the pie cooks.

Bake in a preheated oven at 375°F for 25 minutes until the crust is golden brown and the fruit is tender. (Test with a skewer through the vents in the crust.) Let cool slightly and dust with sifted confectioners' sugar. Mix the cream with the sugar and orange zest and serve with the pie.

key lime pie

The classic key lime pie is made with a graham cracker or cookie crumb crust and topped with whipped cream. My version has a brûlée-style topping and uses my favorite pie crust from the restaurant. You need a deep pie crust to make this tart successfully. When blind baking, put in enough baking beans to come well up the sides, to prevent the dough shrinking back in the pan. The crisp coating hides a velvety smooth and delicate custard with a zingy fresh lime flavor. Use a thin, very sharp knife to cut it, inserting the point first.

1 recipe Old Vic Foolproof Pie Crust (page 63)

1 egg white, for brushing

Lime filling

6 large eggs

¾ cup sugar

finely grated zest and freshly squeezed juice of 10 key limes or 4 regular limes, about ½ cup

2 cups heavy cream

confectioners' sugar, for dusting

a fluted tart pan, 9 inches diameter, 2 inches deep

foil and baking beans or uncooked rice

Serves 6

Make the pie crust dough, line the tart pan, and blind bake in a preheated oven as described on page 63. While still warm, brush the inside of the pie crust with the beaten egg white, then let cool completely. This will seal the crust and keep it crisp when filled. Reduce the oven temperature to 275°F.

To make the lime custard filling, put the eggs and sugar into a bowl and beat with a whisk. Add the grated lime zest and juice. Stir in the cream and chill for about 30 minutes.

Pour the lime custard through a fine strainer and discard the residue. Carefully pour the custard into the cooked pie crust, filling right to the top of the crust. Transfer to the oven and bake for 1–1¼ hours, until the custard is just about set. It will still be slightly wobbly and will continue to set as it cools. Let cool completely on a wire rack.

Transfer to a serving platter and dredge the top thickly with confectioners' sugar. Using a blowtorch, apply direct heat to the sugar until it melts and caramelizes to a deep golden color. When cold, this will form a thin, crisp sugar glaze. A similar effect can be achieved by caramelizing under a hot broiler, but you must cover the edge of the crust with foil to prevent it from burning.

crumbles, cobblers, and betties

Brown betties were very popular in country kitchens during the 19th century. The traditional recipe used apples, but I like the stickiness of the plum juices better.

plum and nutmeg
brown betty

½ cup brown sugar

1¼ lb. very ripe, sweet, juicy plums, halved and pitted

grated zest and juice of 2 limes

½ nutmeg, freshly grated, plus extra, to serve

6 tablespoons unsalted butter

1½ cups fresh brown bread crumbs

1 recipe Quick Vanilla Custard (page 62) or cream, to serve

an ovenproof dish, about 10 inches diameter, greased

Serves 4–6

Reserve 1 tablespoon of the sugar and put the remainder into a bowl. Add the plums, lime zest and juice, grated nutmeg, and 1 tablespoon water and mix well. Set aside to soak for 30 minutes, so the sugar and plums make lots of juice.

Put the butter into a heavy skillet, melt gently, then add the bread crumbs. Cook over medium heat, stirring constantly with a wooden spoon, until all the butter has been absorbed and the crumbs are golden.

Arrange the fruit and crumbs in layers in the prepared dish, finishing with a layer of crumbs. Press down with the back of a spoon to compact the topping, then rough up with a fork and sprinkle with the reserved sugar.

Bake in the middle of a preheated oven at 375°F for 35–45 minutes, until the plums are tender and the top is crisp and brown. (Test the plums with a skewer.)

Serve with custard or cream, sprinkled with a little extra grated nutmeg.

apple cobbler with pecans and maple syrup

The flavors of maple syrup and pecans marry beautifully in this simple dessert. It's important to use a pure, thick maple syrup to give a distinctive toffee flavor. Lighter syrups are certainly cheaper to buy, but bear little resemblance to the real thing.

2¼ lb. crisp red apples, peeled, cored, and thinly sliced

4 tablespoons unsalted butter

1 vanilla bean, split lengthwise and seeds scraped out

1 cup pecans

¼ cup pure maple syrup

1 recipe Quick Vanilla Custard (page 62), to serve

Cobbler topping

1⅔ cups self-rising flour (see page 4)

½ teaspoon salt

3 teaspoons baking powder

4 tablespoons unsalted butter, cut into small pieces

⅔ cup rolled oats, plus 1 tablespoon extra

1 tablespoon sugar

⅔ cup skim milk

1 large egg

a little cream or milk, to glaze

1 tablespoon brown sugar

an ovenproof baking dish, about 10 inches diameter, 2 inches deep

Serves 6–8

Put the prepared apples into a saucepan, add the butter, ⅓ cup water, and the vanilla bean and its seeds. Simmer over a low heat until the juices start to flow and the apples soften, about 10 minutes.

Remove from the heat, then stir in the pecans and syrup. Pour into the baking dish and let cool. Before adding the topping, remove the vanilla bean.

To make the topping, sift the flour, salt, and baking powder into a large bowl. Add the butter and rub in with your fingertips until there are no lumps of butter left and the mixture looks like fine breadcrumbs. Stir in the oats and sugar and make a well in the center. Put the milk and egg into a second bowl and beat well. Add to the well in the flour and oat mixture. Using a table knife, draw the mixture lightly together to form a soft dough.

Turn out onto a floured work surface and lightly knead the dough until smooth underneath. Form into a round shape and press out gently with the flat of your hand to about ½ inch thick. Using a sharp knife, cut the circle in half, then into 6 or 8 wedges. Arrange on top of the fruit with the points facing inward. Brush with a little cream or milk, then sprinkle with the extra oats and brown sugar.

Bake in a preheated oven at 425°F for 5 minutes. Reduce the heat to 400°F and bake for a further 17–20 minutes, or until a skewer inserted into the topping comes out clean. The cobbler should look well risen, crunchy, and golden brown. Serve with vanilla custard.

Rhubarb crumble was one of my grandma's favorites and we ate it warm with custard. Although not, strictly speaking, a crumble, it had a beautifully crisp topping, which we all adored. She used to grow rhubarb in her kitchen garden and would always "force" some under upturned buckets to use in early spring. I loved pulling the long, bright pink stems from the crowns. We would make cones of wax paper, fill them with sugar, then dip in the slender rhubarb stems and nibble them. If you're not a fan of ginger, try finely grated orange zest instead. The two flavors work equally well.

rhubarb crumble
with gingered vanilla

1½ lb. fresh rhubarb

3 pieces of crystallized ginger

½ cup sugar

1 vanilla bean, split lengthwise and seeds scraped out

Crumble topping

1 cup slivered almonds, toasted until lightly golden

6 tablespoons unsalted butter

1 cup brown bread crumbs

¼ cup rolled oats

¼ cup brown sugar

4 individual ovenproof dishes, or a shallow baking dish

Serves 4

Cut the rhubarb into 1-inch pieces. Cut the ginger into thin slices, then crosswise into matchsticks. Put the rhubarb, ginger, sugar, and vanilla bean into a saucepan and cook over gentle heat until the juices run from the rhubarb and it starts to soften. Pour into the ovenproof dishes or baking dish.

To make the topping, put the almonds into a dry skillet and cook, stirring, over gentle heat until lightly golden. Take care or they may burn. Remove and reserve.

Add the butter to the skillet and heat gently until melted. Add the breadcrumbs, oats, and brown sugar. Increase the heat and cook briskly, stirring continuously, until the bread crumbs and oats start to caramelize, brown, and separate. Remove from the skillet and stir in the toasted almonds.

Sprinkle the mixture over the rhubarb, starting at the edges and working towards the middle. Press down firmly. Transfer to a preheated oven and cook at 400°F for about 10 minutes until the topping is crisp and golden (the forced rhubarb is very tender and will finish cooking in this time).

A berry cobbler that's equally good made with raspberries, blackberries, or blueberries. Apples have their own natural sweetness, so less sugar has to be added to the filling. For a light biscuit topping, use your hands to shape the dough (a rolling pin is too heavy for such a light mixture). The walnuts and brown sugar become pleasingly crisp and contrast well with the airy biscuits.

berry and apple crispy cobbler

5 medium red apples

1 lb. berries

1 tablespoon sugar

Cobbler topping

2 cups self-rising flour (see page 4)

½ teaspoon salt

3 teaspoons baking powder

1 tablespoon sugar

4 tablespoons unsalted butter

⅓ cup milk mixed with ⅓ cup water

1 large egg

1 tablespoon light cream

2 tablespoons coarsely chopped walnut pieces

1 tablespoon brown sugar

To serve

confectioners' sugar

whipped cream

an ovenproof baking dish, about 10 inches square, 2 inches deep

a 2-inch fluted cookie cutter

Serves 4–6

Peel, core, and thinly slice the apples. Rinse the berries and pat dry with paper towels. Put the apples and berries into the baking dish, sprinkle with the sugar, and toss gently to coat the fruit in sugar.

To make the topping, sift the flour, salt, and baking powder into a mixing bowl, then stir in the sugar. Cut the butter into small pieces, add to the bowl, and rub in with your fingertips until there are no large lumps of butter and the mixture resembles fine breadcrumbs.

Put the milk and water mixture into a bowl, add the egg, then beat well. Make a well in the flour mixture, then pour in the egg mixture. Using a table knife, draw the mixture lightly together to form a soft dough.

Turn out onto a floured work surface and quickly and lightly knead the dough until smooth. Form into a ball with the sides of your hand and press out evenly and lightly with the flat of your hand to about ½ inch thick. Cut out 8 biscuits with the cookie cutter, then arrange them down the sides or around the edge of the baking dish, on top of the fruit, leaving a space in the center so they will cook evenly. Brush with the cream and sprinkle with the chopped walnuts and brown sugar.

Bake in a preheated oven at 425°F for 5 minutes. Reduce the temperature to 400°F and bake for a further 20 minutes until the biscuits are well risen, golden brown, and crisp with a light, fluffy center.

Dust with confectioners' sugar and serve with whipped cream.

sicilian almond and orange cake

6 extra-large eggs

a pinch of salt

¾ cup plus 2 tablespoons sugar

finely grated zest of 1 orange

1 cup plus 2 tablespoons
all-purpose flour, sifted twice

Filling

1½ lb. ricotta cheese

1 scant cup confectioners'
sugar, sifted

½ cup Cointreau or other
orange liqueur

3 oz. (3 squares) semisweet
chocolate (at least
55–60 percent cocoa
solids), finely chopped

2 tablespoons pistachios,
blanched, peeled, and
coarsely chopped

¼ cup blanched almonds,
coarsely chopped

5 pieces mixed candied fruits,
excess sugar washed off,
dried, and coarsely chopped,
plus extra to serve

Topping

1½ cups heavy cream, whipped
to a soft, floppy consistency

fresh lemon leaves (optional)

*2 sandwich cake pans,
8-inch diameter, greased
and bottom-lined with
parchment paper*

Serves 8–10

This flamboyantly flavored cake with its beautiful topping of candied fruit is almost irresistible. To me, it is the epitome of Sicily: I love the cake almost as much as I love the island.

Put the eggs, salt, and sugar into a large bowl and, using an electric mixer, beat until the mixture doubles in volume and becomes pale and creamy. With the machine still running, gradually beat in 2 tablespoon boiling water—the mixture will thicken considerably and increase in volume. Add the orange zest. Continue beating until the mixture has tripled in volume and, when the beaters are lifted, the mixture leaves a ribbon-like trail on the surface.

Sprinkle half the sifted flour over the surface. Using a metal spoon, carefully and quickly fold in the flour, taking care not to break down the volume. Repeat with the remaining flour. Pour half the mixture into each prepared cake pan and bake in a preheated oven at 350°F for 20–25 minutes until the sponges are golden, well risen and shrinking slightly from the edge of the pans. Transfer to a wire rack and let cool. Carefully peel off the parchment, taking care not to rip the sponge (you may need to use a spatula to help push down the sponge).

To make the filling, put the ricotta into a bowl, then sift in the confectioners' sugar and 3 tablespoons of the liqueur. Beat until light and fluffy. Add the chocolate, nuts, and chopped candied fruit and fold into the mixture.

To assemble, put one sponge, top side down, onto a large plate. Sprinkle 2 tablespoons liqueur over the surface and let soak for a few minutes. Spread the filling over the top. Sprinkle the underside of the second sponge with 1 tablespoon liqueur, then put on top of the filling. Finally, sprinkle the top of the cake with the remaining liqueur. Cover and chill for 2–3 hours.

To finish, spread the whipped cream over the top and sides of the cake with a spatula. Top with the whole candied fruit pieces and lemon leaves, if using.

chocolate truffle cake
with caramelized pecans

This dark, smooth, meltingly rich chocolate cake is perfect for dinner parties—the smallest slice will satisfy even the grandest appetite.

7 oz. plain chocolate wafer cookies

6 tablespoons unsalted butter

1 cup pecans, lightly toasted and chopped

1 square (1 oz.) bittersweet chocolate (at least 55–60 percent cocoa solids), melted

a pinch of ground cinnamon

Truffle filling

½ cup pecans

½ cup confectioners' sugar

2⅓ cups heavy cream

2 packages (1 lb.) bittersweet chocolate (at least 55–60 percent cocoa solids)

Topping

2–2½ cups pecan halves

⅔ cup confectioners' sugar

1 tablespoon unsweetened cocoa powder

a springform cake pan, 8-inch diameter, greased

a baking sheet, lightly oiled

Serves 8–10

To make the cookie base, put the chocolate cookies into a blender or food processor and blend until finely crushed. Put the butter into a small saucepan and melt gently. Add the cookie crumbs, chopped nuts, melted chocolate, and cinnamon. Mix well. Pour the mixture into the prepared cake pan and, using the back of a spoon, firmly press down to cover the base of the pan. Chill well.

To make the filling, put the pecans into a heavy skillet and cover with the confectioners' sugar. Cook over a medium heat, stirring occasionally, until the sugar dissolves and turns into a deep caramel which coats the nuts. Pour onto the prepared baking sheet and let cool until hard. Break into pieces. Transfer to a food processor and blend until fine.

Put the cream into a bowl and whip until soft peaks form. Chop the chocolate, put into a heatproof bowl set over a saucepan of simmering water, and melt gently. Do not let any water or steam touch the chocolate. Let cool slightly.

Fold the melted chocolate into the whipped cream until smooth, then fold in the processed caramelized nuts. Pour the mixture over the cookie base in the prepared pan. Tap the pan on the work surface a few times to level the mixture and remove any trapped air bubbles. Cover and chill in the refrigerator for at least 4–5 hours, preferably overnight.

To make the topping, put the pecans into a skillet, sprinkle with confectioners' sugar, and caramelize, harden, and cool as before. Remove the cake from the pan and transfer to a serving plate. If using cocoa, sift it thickly over the top and arrange the caramelized pecans in a circle around the edge of the cake.

This very simple yet elegant cheesecake needs no fruit for embellishment. However, a few chocolate curls or "caraques" resting on the glossy sour cream glaze look wonderful.

baked lemon and chocolate cheesecake

11 oz. plain chocolate wafer cookies

1 stick unsalted butter

¾ cup chopped walnuts

1 square (1 oz.) bittersweet chocolate (at least 55–60 percent cocoa solids), finely chopped

Filling

2 cups (1 lb.) cream cheese

finely grated zest and juice of 2 lemons

1 vanilla bean, split lengthwise and seeds scraped out

3 extra-large eggs

1 cup sugar

Topping

⅓ cup sour cream

a little freshly grated nutmeg

Chocolate Caraques (curls or quills)*

confectioners' sugar, for dusting

a false-bottom tart pan, 10 inches diameter

Serves 8

To make the cookie base, put the chocolate cookies into a blender or food processor and process until finely crushed.

Put the butter into a saucepan and melt over a gentle heat. Stir in the cookie crumb mixture, chopped walnuts, and chopped chocolate. Heat until melted and well mixed, about 2–3 minutes.

Pour the cookie mixture into the tart pan and, using the back of a spoon, firmly press down to cover the base and sides of the pan evenly. Chill well.

To make the filling, put the cream cheese, lemon zest and juice, and vanilla seeds into a large, shallow bowl and beat until light and smooth. Put the eggs and sugar into a separate bowl and, using an electric mixer, beat until the mixture thickens and when the beaters are lifted the mixture leaves a ribbon-like trail on the surface. Using a whisk, gently fold the egg mixture into the cream cheese mixture, until blended but still light and fluffy. Pour into the prepared cookie crust.

Bake in a preheated oven at 275°F for about 30–35 minutes until only just set: the cheesecake will continue cooking as it cools.

While the cheesecake is still slightly warm, pour the sour cream over the top of the filling—it will set and become very glossy. When the cheesecake is completely cool, sprinkle with a little freshly grated nutmeg. Top with the chocolate caraques and dust with confectioners' sugar just before serving.

*Chocolate Caraques Pour melted chocolate onto a chopping board and let set. Using a long knife, and working away from you, slowly scrape over the chocolate. The chocolate will curl into quills.

strawberry cheesecake

This light, fruity, uncooked cheesecake is perfect for a summer's day—thanks to packaged gelatin, it is simple and easy to make.

8 oz. shortbread cookies

4 tablespoons unsalted butter

Strawberry cheese filling

1¼ lb. strawberries, washed, dried, and hulled

grated zest and juice of ½ lemon

1½ packages powdered gelatin (¼ oz. each)

8 oz. package cream cheese, about 1 cup

½ cup sugar

1 vanilla bean, split lengthwise and seeds scraped out

2 tablespoons plain yogurt

⅔ cup heavy cream

1 large egg white

a pinch of salt

a few sprigs of mint, to serve (optional)

a springform or deep false-bottom cake pan, 7 inches diameter, lightly buttered

Serves 6–8

Put the cookies into a blender or food processor and blend until finely crushed. Melt the butter in a small saucepan. Add the cookie crumbs and mix well. Pour the buttered crumbs into the prepared pan and, using the back of a spoon, firmly press them down to cover the base. Bake in a preheated oven at 350° for 8–10 minutes, then remove from the oven and let cool.

Cut about 10 small strawberries in half and reserve for later. Put the rest into a bowl. Add the lemon zest and juice and crush lightly with a fork, making sure the strawberries are still chunky.

Put 3 tablespoons hot (but not boiling) water into a heatproof bowl, then sprinkle in the gelatin. Let stand for about 5 minutes, then put into a saucepan of water and heat gently, stirring until the gelatin completely dissolves.

Put the cream cheese into a bowl and beat until soft. Add the sugar, vanilla seeds, yogurt, and cream and beat until the mixture is smooth and fluffy. Fold in the crushed strawberry mixture.

Mix a spoonful of the strawberry cheese mixture into the gelatin to lighten it, then steadily pour back into the strawberry cheese mixture, stirring constantly as you pour, until well mixed.

Beat the egg white and salt until stiff peaks form, then fold into the strawberry cheese mixture and pour on top of the cookie base in the pan. Tap the pan on the work surface a few times to let the mixture settle and to level the surface. Cover and chill in the refrigerator for at least 2–3 hours until set.

To serve, turn out onto a serving plate, top with the reserved strawberries and a sprig or two of mint, if using.

boston cream pie

A New England classic, this is really a cake, not a pie, and is usually thicker than the one I make. I think the apricot purée adds clarity and freshness, but it also isn't traditional. To make chocolate leaves, paint the underside of unsprayed rose leaves with melted chocolate and let cool. When completely set, carefully peel away the leaves to reveal perfect chocolate replicas.

1 tablespoon unsalted butter

⅓ cup milk

2 large eggs

1 cup plus 1 tablespoon sugar

½ teaspoon vanilla extract

½ cup all-purpose flour

1 teaspoon baking powder

a pinch of salt

Filling

1¾ cups milk

4 large egg yolks

1 vanilla bean, split lengthwise
and seeds scraped out

2 tablespoons cornstarch

¼ cup sugar

3 canned apricot halves,
in natural juice

Topping

4 oz. (4 squares) semisweet
chocolate (at least
55–60 percent cocoa solids)

2 tablespoons unsalted butter

1 tablespoon strong
black coffee

chocolate leaves (optional—
see recipe introduction)

*a deep cake pan, 8 inches
diameter, greased, floured
and bottom-lined with
parchment paper*

Serves 6–8

To make the sponge, put the butter and milk into a small saucepan and heat gently until the butter has melted. Keep the mixture warm.

Using an electric mixer, beat the eggs, sugar, and vanilla in a large bowl until pale, thick, and creamy and the mixture leaves a ribbon-like trail when the beaters are lifted. Sift the flour, baking powder, and salt over the mixture in 2 batches. Using a large metal spoon, fold in the first batch, then the second.

Trickle the warmed butter and milk mixture around the edge of the sponge mixture, near the sides of the bowl, then gently fold in to make a smooth batter. Pour into the prepared cake pan and bake in a preheated oven at 350°F for 25–30 minutes until well risen, the sponge has shrunk slightly from the sides, and a skewer inserted in the middle comes out clean.

Let cool in the pan for 5 minutes, then turn out onto a wire rack and let cool completely. Peel off the parchment paper and slice the cake into 2 layers.

To make the filling, put the milk into a saucepan and slowly bring it to a boil. Put the egg yolks, vanilla seeds, cornstarch, and sugar into a bowl, mix well, then beat into the hot milk. Strain the mixture, then pour back into the pan and return to the heat. Simmer for 3–4 minutes, beating vigorously until smooth and thick. Remove, put plastic wrap over the surface to prevent a skin forming and let cool. Chill.

Put the apricots into a blender and work to a purée, adding a little juice from the can to loosen the mixture if necessary.

To make the topping, melt the chocolate, butter, and coffee in a heatproof bowl set over a saucepan of simmering water. Mix until glossy and smooth.

To assemble the cake, put one sponge layer on a serving plate and spread the filling on top, up to the edges. Dot 3 tablespoons of the apricot purée over the filling and swirl with the tip of a small knife.

Put the second sponge layer on top of the filling. Spread the chocolate topping over the sandwiched cake, chill until almost set, then add the chocolate leaves, if using, and serve.

The taste and texture of this beautiful cake actually improve over a day or two, as the flavors develop and intensify. If you can't find framboise (raspberry liqueur), try Kirsch instead.

rich chocolate cake
with raspberries and framboise cream

1 package (8 oz.) semisweet chocolate (at least 55–60 percent cocoa solids), chopped

¼ cup dark rum

4 extra-large eggs, separated

½ cup sugar, plus extra for sprinkling

a pinch of salt

Raspberry filling

2⅔ cups heavy cream

1 tablespoon sugar

2 tablespoons framboise (raspberry liqueur) or Kirsch

1 lb. raspberries, about 3 cups

confectioners' sugar, for dusting

tiny sprigs of mint, to serve

3 cake pans, 8-inch diameter, greased and bottom-lined with parchment paper

wax paper

Serves 8–10

Put the chocolate and rum into a heatproof bowl set over a saucepan of simmering water and heat until melted.

Put the egg yolks and sugar into a large bowl and, using an electric mixer, beat until the mixture doubles in volume, becomes thick and creamy, and leaves a ribbon-like trail on the surface when the beaters are lifted. Fold in the melted rum and chocolate mixture.

Put the egg whites and salt into a bowl and beat until stiff peaks form.

Gently fold into the chocolate mixture, in 3 batches, taking care not to break down the volume of the mixture. Divide the mixture evenly between the prepared cake pans and bake in a preheated oven at 350°F for 15–20 minutes until risen, the sponge has shrunk slightly from the sides, and a skewer inserted in the middle comes out clean. The cakes will have a cracked surface.

Lay large sheets of wax paper on 2 wire racks and sprinkle with a thin layer of sugar. Turn out the cakes onto the sugared wax paper and let cool.

To make the filling, put the cream, sugar, and framboise into a bowl and lightly whip until soft peaks form. Reserve about ⅔ cup of the raspberries for serving and gently fold the rest into the whipped cream.

Sandwich the raspberry cream filling evenly between the 3 chocolate sponges to make a layered cake. Top with the reserved raspberries. Sift confectioners' sugar over the berries and the cake, then add sprigs of mint and serve.

gelatins, soufflés,
and meringues

hazelnut lemon meringue cake

This lovely, chewy, nutty-flavored meringue is very easy to make. Don't over-grind the hazelnuts, as this releases the nut oils and makes the meringue heavy. Making lemon curd is a good way of using the spare yolks from this cake and the sharp lemony flavor marries particularly well with the sweetness of the meringue. Extra yolks have many uses.

6 extra-large egg whites

a pinch of salt

2 cups sugar

⅔ cup skinned hazelnuts, toasted in a dry skillet, then coarsely ground

1 cup heavy cream, lightly whipped to soft peaks

½ cup Lemon Curd (see page 62)

1 tablespoon confectioners' sugar, for dusting

2 baking sheets, lined with parchment paper and marked with a 8-inch circle

long metal skewers

Serves 8–10

Put the egg whites and salt into a large, clean, greasefree bowl and beat with an electric mixer until soft peaks form. Using a large metal spoon, fold in ¾ cup of the sugar. Beat again until glossy and stiff. Repeat once more with the remaining sugar.

Sprinkle the ground hazelnuts over the top, then carefully and lightly fold into the meringue—take care not to break down the volume of the mixture.

Divide the nut meringue between the 2 prepared trays and spread the mixture to fill each marked circle.

Bake in a preheated oven at 325°F for about 1¼–1½ hours, swapping the trays halfway through cooking, until crisp on the outside and soft in the middle. Remove from the oven and let cool. Alternatively, for a crisper meringue, switch off the oven and leave the meringues inside for about 2 hours, then remove. When completely cold, carefully peel off the parchment paper and put one meringue onto a serving plate. Spread the whipped cream over the top, then the lemon curd. Top with the second meringue, set upside down.

Sift the confectioners' sugar over the top of the layered meringue. Heat several long metal skewers until red hot, then use to make crisscross patterns on top: the heat from the skewers will caramelize the sugar.

chocolate and tia maria soufflé

1 package (8 oz.) semisweet chocolate, chopped

2 tablespoons coffee liqueur

4 extra-large egg whites

a pinch of salt

¼ cup sugar

confectioners' sugar, for dusting

4 soufflé dishes or ramekins, ½ cup each, about 3 inches diameter, lightly greased and dusted with sugar

Serves 4

Gently melt the chocolate in a heatproof bowl set over a saucepan of simmering water, stirring with a spatula. Let cool a little—it must be liquid when added to the egg whites. Pour 1 tablespoon of the chocolate and ½ tablespoon of the coffee liqueur into each soufflé dish.

Put the egg whites and salt into a large, clean, greasefree bowl and beat until stiff. Add 1 teaspoon of the sugar and beat until glossy and stiff. Add half the remaining sugar and beat back to stiff peaks. Repeat with the remaining sugar.

Using a balloon whisk, gently and quickly fold the melted chocolate into the whites. Pour the mixture into the soufflé dishes and bake immediately in a preheated oven at 425°F for 4–5 minutes until well risen and crusty on top. Dust lightly with confectioners' sugar and serve immediately.

apricot and orange soufflé

Coarsely chop 3 of the apricots and divide between the prepared soufflé dishes. Finely grate the orange zest and divide half between the soufflé dishes.

Put the remaining apricots and orange zest into a blender or food processor. Add the egg yolks, vanilla seeds, cream, lemon juice, sugar, and flour. Purée until smooth.

Put the egg whites into a large, clean, greasefree bowl. Using an electric hand-held mixer, beat until soft peaks form. Sift the cream of tartar on top and beat again until stiff peaks form. Using a large metal spoon, fold the purée into the beaten egg whites, taking care not to break down the volume. Pour into the prepared dishes. Run your thumb around the inside edge of each dish.

Bake in a preheated oven at 400°F for 10–12 minutes, until the soufflés are well risen and golden brown. Dust with confectioners' sugar and serve.

15 oz. canned apricots in juice, about 2 cups, well drained

2 oranges

3 large eggs, separated

1 vanilla bean, split lengthwise

2 tablespoons heavy cream

1 teaspoon freshly squeezed lemon juice

2 tablespoons sugar

2 tablespoons all-purpose flour

½ teaspoon cream of tartar

confectioners' sugar, for dusting

6 soufflé dishes, 3 inches diameter, prepared as in the previous recipe

Serves 6

Preparing soufflés need not be intimidating—just make sure that the transition from the mixing bowl to the dining table is smooth and without interruption. Serve as soon as they come out of the oven.

strawberry and vanilla fool

Fools are easy and delicious desserts. You can use any soft fruit—or even crisp ones, if you cook them to to a soft purée first.

1 lb. strawberries

2 tablespoons confectioners' sugar

1 vanilla bean, split lengthwise, seeds scraped out

1 cup heavy cream

2 teaspoons vanilla sugar (see note page 4)

½ recipe Quick Vanilla Custard, using 3 egg yolks, well chilled (page 62)

6 glasses

Serves 6

Reserve a few small strawberries for serving. Put the rest into a blender or food processor, add the confectioners' sugar, blend to a purée, then pour into a bowl. Add the vanilla bean and seeds to the strawberry mixture and chill for an hour or so to infuse. Press through a fine nylon strainer to make a smooth, thick purée.

Put the cream and vanilla sugar into a bowl. Beat until thick and floppy. Chill.

To serve, fill the serving glasses with alternate layers of vanilla custard, strawberry purée, and vanilla cream. Swirl together using a toothpick, skewer, or small pointed knife to give a marbled effect. Cut the reserved strawberries in half, add to the glasses, then serve chilled.

raspberry cranachan

A traditional Scottish dessert using local ingredients—Scotch whiskey, heather honey, raspberries, and oatmeal.

Put the oatmeal into a dry skillet and toast gently until dry. Add the sugar and continue toasting until the oatmeal is golden and caramelized. Let cool.

Put the cream and honey into a bowl, beat until thick, then fold in the whiskey. Set aside a few small, perfect raspberries for serving. Fold the remainder into the cream mixture, then taste and add a little more honey if needed.

Layer the whiskey raspberry cream in glasses in alternate layers with the crunchy oatmeal. Top with the reserved raspberries and serve well chilled.

½ cup coarse oatmeal

1 tablespoon brown sugar

1¼ cups heavy cream

1 tablespoon light honey

⅓ cup Scotch whiskey

8 oz. fresh raspberries, about 1½ cups

6 glasses

Serves 6

To produce a crystal clear, shimmering gelatin, it is important to use leaf gelatin: happily, it is also simplicity itself to handle. To be truly sophisticated, worthy of any elegant dinner party, the gelatin must be light and wobbly without a trace of stiffness.

blackberry port gelatin
with vanilla and port syrup

8 oz. blackberries, about 1½ cups

½ cup sugar

juice of ½ lemon

⅔ cup late-bottled vintage port

4 thin sheets of leaf gelatin

Vanilla and port syrup

½ cup sugar

1 vanilla bean, split lengthwise and seeds scraped out

3 large blackberries

To serve

a few blackberries

confectioners' sugar, for dusting

4–6 sprigs of mint (optional)

4–6 individual molds, wetted with water—simple shapes work best, such as small ramekins or soufflé dishes

Serves 4–6

To make the jelly, put the blackberries into a saucepan, add 1¼ cups cold water, the sugar, lemon juice, and port, bring to a boil, and simmer gently until tender. Press through a nylon strainer to remove all the seeds.

Put the leaf gelatin into a bowl and cover with cold water. Leave for 10 minutes to soften, then drain and squeeze the leaves with your hand to remove excess water before stirring them into the warm fruit liquid. Stir until completely dissolved. Pour the mixture into the wetted molds and let set in the refrigerator.

To make the syrup, put ½ cup water into a saucepan, add the sugar, and dissolve over a low heat. Increase the heat and bring to a boil. Add the split vanilla bean, vanilla seeds, and blackberries and simmer until reduced by half to make a thick syrup. Press through a fine nylon strainer, pushing through the blackberry flesh, but retaining the seeds and vanilla bean in the strainer. (You will now have a pink blush-colored syrup flavored heavily with vanilla.) Chill well.

When ready to serve, dip the base of the molds very briefly in hot water and turn out the gelatins onto serving plates. Top with a pile of berries, a pool of vanilla syrup, a light dusting of confectioners' sugar, and a sprig of mint, if using.

A pinch of salt added to the egg whites increases the volume and stabilizes the foam, so the meringue holds its shape better, while the combination of lemon juice, cornstarch, and sugar gives the meringue a thick marshmallow center, so typical of pavlova. The sweetness of the meringue is offset by the sharpness of the fruit. In Australia, the home of pavlova, other fruits are used, such as strawberries and tropical fruit, so feel free to vary the recipe using whatever is sweet and ripe—and in season. Passionfruit, however, is almost mandatory.

raspberry and passionfruit pavlova

4 extra-large egg whites

a pinch of salt

1¾ cups sugar

1 tablespoon cornstarch

2 teaspoons lemon juice

Filling

1⅓ cups heavy cream

10 oz. raspberries, about 2 cups

3–4 passionfruit

Raspberry purée

6 oz. raspberries, about 1½ cups

1–2 tablespoons confectioners' sugar, sifted

a baking sheet, lined with parchment paper and sprinkled with cornstarch

Serves 6–8

Put the egg whites and salt into a large bowl. Using an electric mixer, beat the egg whites until stiff. Gradually add ⅔ cup of the sugar, beating between each addition until the meringue is very glossy and stiff. Beat in the remaining ⅓ cup sugar (reserving the extra tablespoon).

Sift the reserved sugar and cornstarch together into a small bowl and mix well. Fold half the cornstarch mixture into the meringue, then 1 teaspoon of the lemon juice. Repeat.

Spoon half the meringue onto the parchment paper and spread out to a disk about 7 inches in diameter. Smooth the top and sides. Spoon the rest of the meringue in a ring around the edge of the circle of meringue until the pavlova is about 2½ inches thick.

Bake in a preheated oven at 250°F for about 1–1¼ hours. Remove from the oven and let cool. Alternatively, switch off the oven and leave the meringue inside until cool. This will help reduce cracking.

To make the raspberry purée, crush the raspberries with a fork or hand-held immersion blender, then press through a nylon strainer to make a purée. Discard the seeds. Mix in enough of the confectioners' sugar to sweeten to taste.

When the pavlova is cold, carefully remove the parchment paper and put the pavlova onto a serving plate. Fill the center with the whipped cream and top with the raspberries. Cut the passionfruit in half and scoop out the pulp and seeds onto the raspberries. Serve decorated with a few sprigs of mint and the raspberry purée.

basic recipes

lemon curd

Unwaxed lemons are best for recipes using lemon zest, but, if you can't find them, soak the lemons in very hot water first to melt the wax, then dry thoroughly before starting on the recipe.

finely grated zest and juice of 3 unwaxed lemons
1¼ sticks unsalted butter
⅔ cup sugar
6 large egg yolks, beaten

Makes about 2 cups

Put the lemon zest, juice, and butter into a heatproof bowl set over a saucepan of simmering water or in the top of a double boiler. Heat gently until the butter has melted and the sugar has dissolved.

Remove from the heat, add the beaten egg yolks and mix well. Return to the heat and cook gently, stirring constantly until thickened. The curd should be thick enough to coat the back of a spoon and leave a trail when lifted.

Pass through a fine strainer to remove any bits of zest or lemon pulp. Use to fill meringues, cakes, or sandwiches or, alternatively, pour into a sterilized jar (see page 4) and refrigerate until needed. Use within 1 month.

quick vanilla custard

Using cornstarch to stabilize custard may not please the purists, but it works perfectly and prevents any possibility of curdling.

5 large egg yolks
1 teaspoon cornstarch
2 tablespoons sugar
1 vanilla bean
2¾ cups heavy cream

Serves 4–6

Put the egg yolks, cornstarch, and sugar into a mixing bowl and beat well.

Split the vanilla bean lengthwise and scrape out the seeds. Put the seeds and cream into a saucepan and bring to a boil. When the cream rises in the pan, quickly pour it onto the egg mixture, beating vigorously and continuously, until the custard thickens.

old vic foolproof pie crust

This pie crust is named after my restaurant, the Old Vicarage. It is used in a number of the recipes in this book. You can't go wrong with it, provided you follow the method exactly.

1 large egg

1 teaspoon freshly squeezed lemon juice

1 cup plus 2 tablespoons all-purpose flour

a pinch of salt

1 teaspoon confectioners' sugar

1 stick plus 2 tablespoons unsalted butter, diced

foil and baking beans or uncooked rice

Makes about 12 oz.

(see note below right)

Put the egg and lemon juice into a bowl, add 2 tablespoons ice water, and beat well. Chill until needed—the mixture will thicken slightly.

Sift the flour, salt, and confectioners' sugar into a mixing bowl. Add the butter and rub in with your fingertips until the mixture is crumbly but rough. Don't try to rub it in finely at this stage. Make a well in the center and add the egg liquid. Using a round-bladed knife, bring the mixture together to form a dough. (Use a cutting action rather than a stirring action or the dough will become tough when cooked.)

Transfer to a lightly floured surface and knead briefly until the dough is smooth, like putty. Wrap in plastic wrap and let rest in the refrigerator for at least 30 minutes before using. Roll out to a shape just larger than the pie dish or tart pan you will be using.

Blind Baking If the recipe tells you to bake the pie crust dough blind, after rolling out the dough, use the pin to help you lift it, then carefully lower it into the tart pan. Ease it evenly up the sides of the pan, taking care not to trap air between the dough and the pan. Take particular care where the sides meet the base. Prick the base of the pie crust dough with a fork.

Line with aluminum foil and fill with baking beans or uncooked rice. Bake in a preheated oven at 350°F for about 15 minutes. Remove the foil and beans and return the pie crust to the oven for a further 5 minutes to dry out and cook through. Fill as described in the recipe chosen.

Dough Quantity The quantity of dough given here is enough for one large tart, 8 inches in diameter, or 6 tartlets, 4 inches diameter. For a deep, double-crusted pie, 10 inches diameter, such as the Old-Fashioned Apple Pie on page 19, double the ingredients. There is no need to make 2 separate batches.

index

conversion chart

Weights and measures have been rounded up or down slightly to make measuring easier.

Volume equivalents:

American	Metric	Imperial
1 teaspoon	5 ml	
1 tablespoon	15 ml	
¼ cup	60 ml	2 fl.oz.
⅓ cup	75 ml	2½ fl.oz.
½ cup	125 ml	4 fl.oz.
⅔ cup	150 ml	5 fl.oz. (¼ pint)
¾ cup	175 ml	6 fl.oz.
1 cup	250 ml	8 fl.oz.

Weight equivalents: **Measurements:**

Imperial	Metric	Inches	Cm
1 oz.	25 g	¼ inch	5 mm
2 oz.	50 g	½ inch	1 cm
3 oz.	75 g	¾ inch	1.5 cm
4 oz.	125 g	1 inch	2.5 cm
5 oz.	150 g	2 inches	5 cm
6 oz.	175 g	3 inches	7 cm
7 oz.	200 g	4 inches	10 cm
8 oz. (½ lb.)	250 g	5 inches	12 cm
9 oz.	275 g	6 inches	15 cm
10 oz.	300 g	7 inches	18 cm
11 oz.	325 g	8 inches	20 cm
12 oz.	375 g	9 inches	23 cm
13 oz.	400 g	10 inches	25 cm
14 oz.	425 g	11 inches	28 cm
15 oz.	475 g	12 inches	30 cm
16 oz. (1 lb.)	500 g		
2 1b.	1 kg		

Oven temperatures:

110°C	(225°F)	Gas ¼
120°C	(250°F)	Gas ½
140°C	(275°F)	Gas 1
150°C	(300°F)	Gas 2
160°C	(325°F)	Gas 3
180°C	(350°F)	Gas 4
190°C	(375°F)	Gas 5
200°C	(400°F)	Gas 6
220°C	(425°F)	Gas 7
230°C	(450°F)	Gas 8
240°C	(475°F)	Gas 9